M000091976

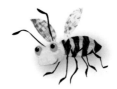

Can It Fit?

by Lada Josefa Kratky

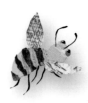

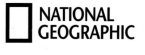
NATIONAL GEOGRAPHIC

School Publishing

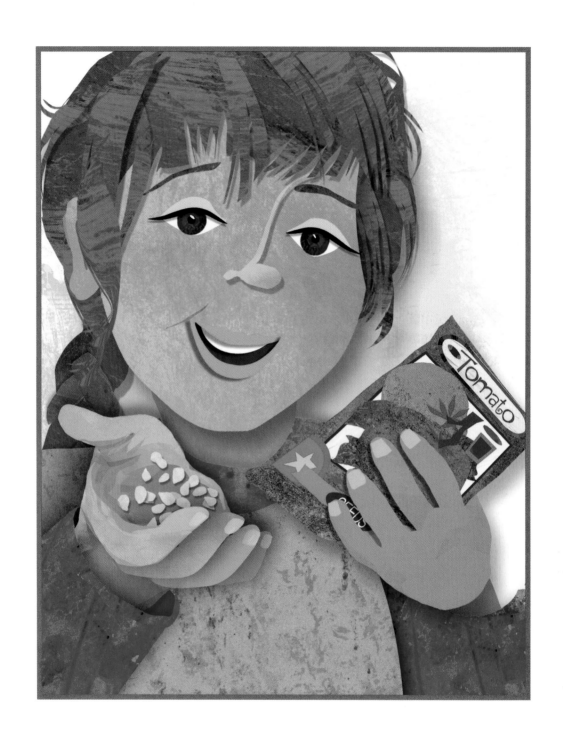

See this? Look!

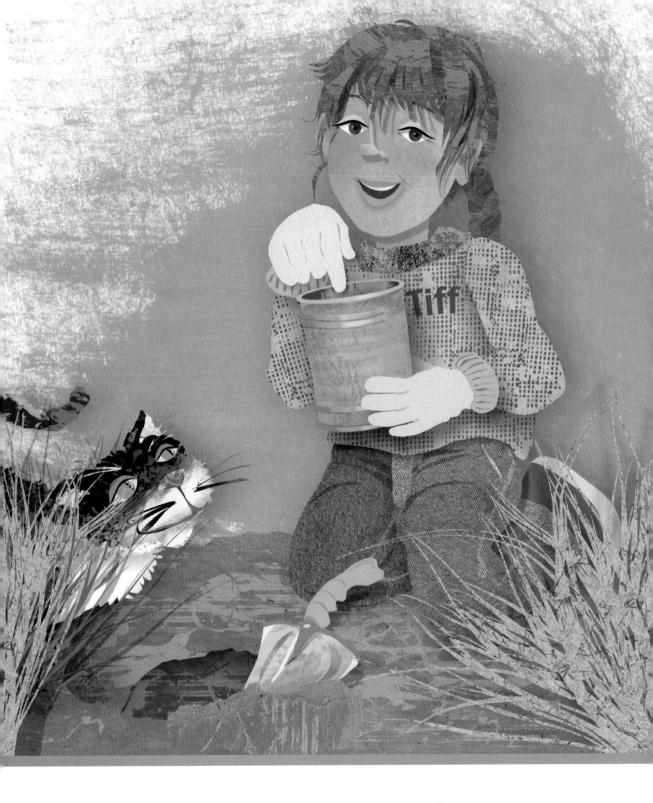

This is a can for it.

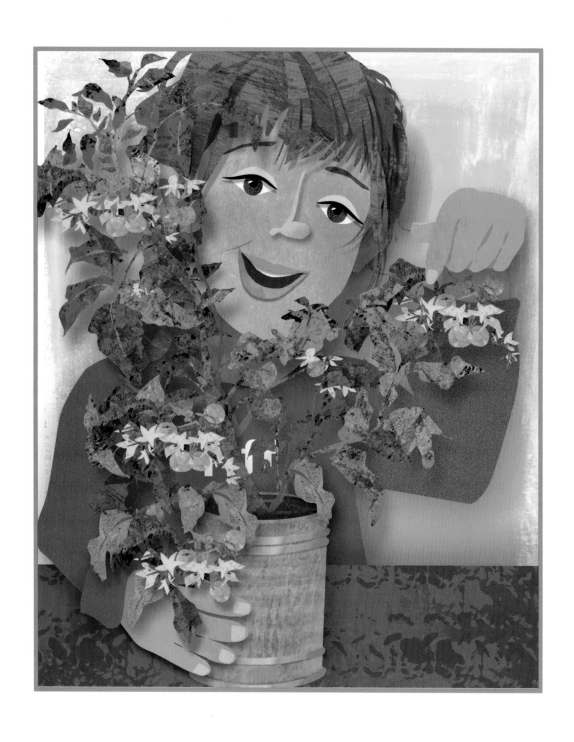

See this? Look!

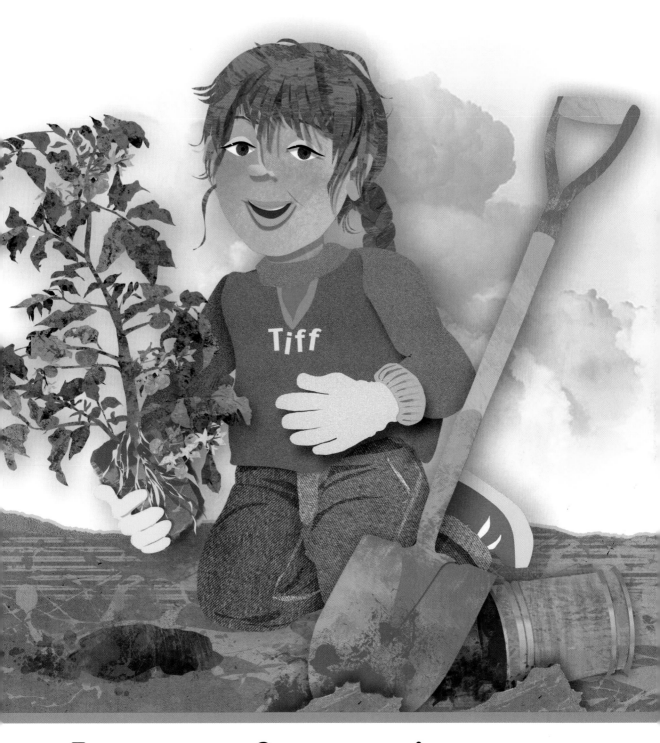

It can fit in the pit.

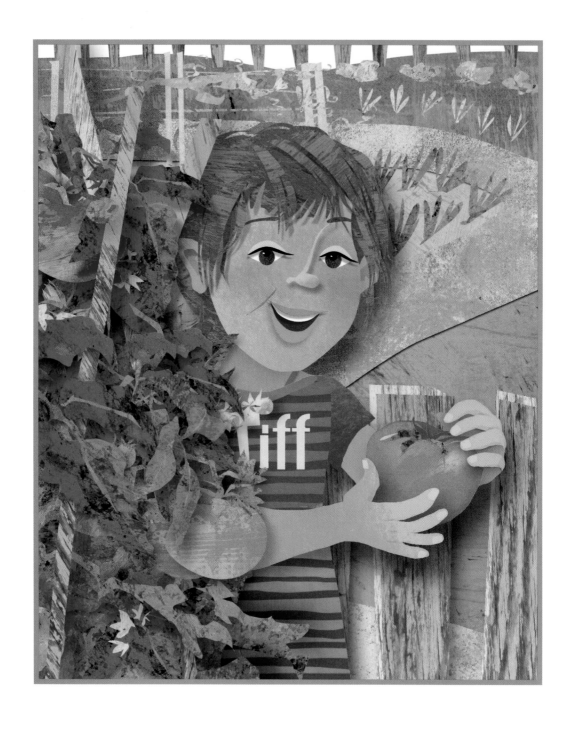

See this? It is fat.

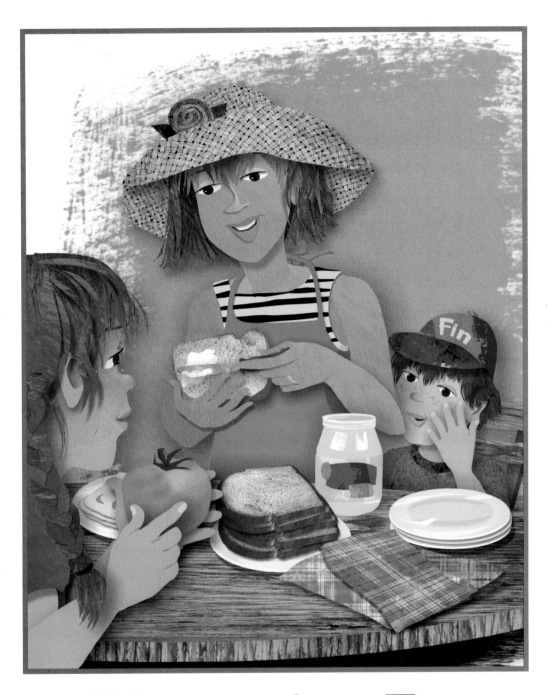

This is for Fin.
Can it fit in?

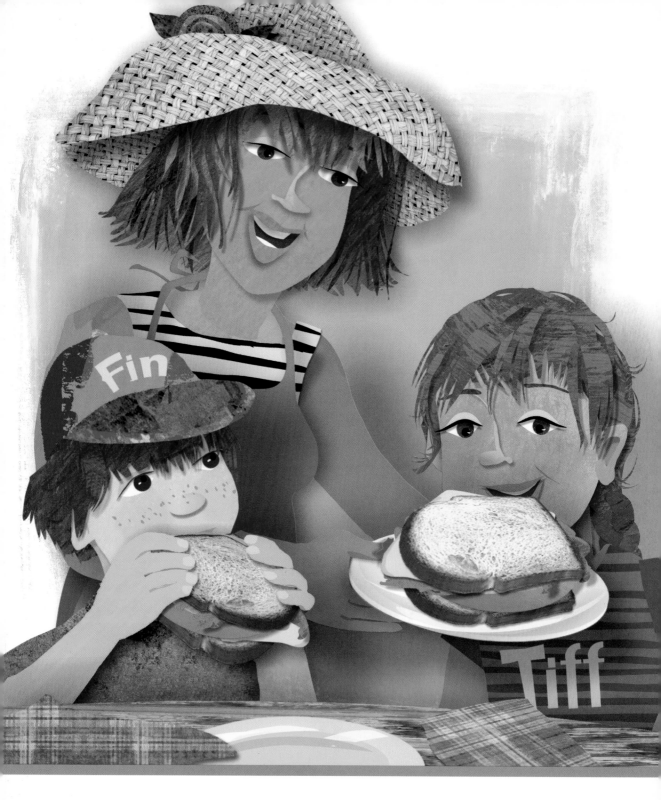

It can. This is for Tiff.